POT LUCK
Potato Recipes from Ireland

'The humble spud does the honours in this mouth-watering
collection of recipes that'll leave you positively
gobsmacked at the number of things you can do with an
ordinary potato!' *Sunday World*

'A handy little book for the kitchen shelf.'
Inside Ireland

'Potato soups, stews, chowders, salads, oven-baked
and oven-top dishes combine to make the
humble tuber sound tastier than ever ...
an imaginative yet simple recipe for every occasion.'
Cork Examiner

Dedication

To my mother, Mary Gorman Schofield, with loving memory. She welcomed all her daughters into her busy kitchen at an early age. We loved every moment of our time spent in creative and messy experimentation.

POT LUCK
Potato Recipes from Ireland

Nell Donnelly

with illustrations by
Jimmy Burns

WOLFHOUND PRESS

This new edition published in 2005 by
Wolfhound Press
An Imprint of Merlin Publishing
16 Upper Pembroke Street
Dublin 2, Ireland
Tel: +353 1 676 4373
Fax: +353 1 676 4368
publishing@merlin.ie
www.merlinwolfhound.com

First published 1987
Reprinted 1990, 1992, 1994, 1995, 1997, 1998, 2001
Second edition 2005

ISBN 0-86327-933-3

A CIP catalogue record for this book is available from the British Library.

5 4 3 2 1

Publisher's Acknowledgements
The proverbs, verses, songs and poems have been taken from two main
sources which we hereby acknowledge: *Proverbs and Sayings of Ireland*,
Seán Gaffney and Seamus Cashman (1974, Wolfhound Press) and *An
Anthology of the Potato*, Robert McKay (1961, Allen Figgis & Co Ltd,
for the Irish Potato Marketing Company Ltd, Dublin)

Cover Design by Graham Thew Design
Typesetting by Redsetter Ltd
Printed and bound by J H Haynes & Co Ltd, Britain

CONTENTS

SOUPS, STEWS AND CHOWDERS

SALADS

OVEN-BAKED DISHES

SKILLET RECIPES

BAKED JACKET POTATOES

POT LUCK

DESSERT

INTRODUCTION

Throughout the ages cooks everywhere have learned to use the humble potato in a great variety of ways. They've been boiled, baked, grilled, grated and garnished. Today the spud is a dietary mainstay, recognised for its high nutritive value.

The recipes in this book utilize many different ingredients which, when properly combined with the potato, produce dishes of truly dramatic proportions. This book will provide the family cook with a wealth of great recipes for soups, stews, chowders, salads (hot and cold), pot luck, skillet or frying pan cooking and many delicious oven-baked wonders; all are quite easy to prepare and all provide exceptional value for money.

The savoury odour from the kitchen as these hot and cold dishes are being prepared is guaranteed to delight even the most discriminating palate and it is my pleasure to pass these recipes along to you so that you too may enjoy the many mouth-watering delights that have been handed down through the generations of my family to me.

As you build your own favourites from these pages, I know you will make use of them often. Some undoubtedly will be served more frequently when there are guests to help with the eating. For the hurried cook there are many gourmet short-cuts that put today's instant mixes and sauces to imaginative use. The preparation of these dishes is certainly easy and the results are always appetizing. Perhaps you will be able to impart some of your own culinary magic to yield a distinctively personal dish. Aided by the potato the world of good food is yours.

Nell Donnelly

BUT AREN'T THEY FATTENING?

No other foodstuff is so maligned as the potato when in fact it produces more than its fair share of major nutrients. Nutritionists have pointed out that a large uncooked apple contains more calories than a medium-sized potato. The potato is about 80% water and 20% solid matter and when the water is removed, about 10% of the remaining solids is protein. In addition, with only the barest trace of fat, the spud is high in vitamin C, necessary for healthy gums, muscles, skin and bones. Other essential vitamins in the potato are A and B_1 with riboflavin, thiamin and niacin, all factors of the vitamin B complex. It is also a source of fibre, an essential component in any diet.

A medium-sized potato (boiled and unpeeled) provides the following:

120 calories
3 grams of protein
27 grams of carbohydrates

All the food nutrients necessary in a human diet would be met by eating 5 lbs. of potatoes and drinking a quart of milk a day. It was not uncommon in old Ireland to raise a family of 10 children on a diet consisting of potatoes and buttermilk with an occasional fish or egg added for variety.

The tuber is an invaluable source of necessary minerals, vital in the promotion of good health, including phosphorus, magnesium, sodium, iodine, zinc and copper. With trace elements of these minerals and its rich vitamin content, is it any wonder the potato remains an important part of our national diet?

THE HISTORY OF THE POTATO

It may be difficult to imagine, but the potato has a history as checkered as a tablecloth in a fine Italian restaurant, peppered with claims, off-setting claims, evidence and counter-evidence. Horticulturalists and botanists have battled over the potato's origins, its method of reaching Europe, and the individual responsible for its reaching these shores.

Even today the quiet controversy continues behind hallowed ivy-covered academic walls as to where and when and who, while the subject in question, *solanum tuberosum* or the humble potato, still tickles the palates of millions throughout the world, and at the same time enjoys a unique place in the history of art, poetry, song, literature, medicine and even the course of history.

But first, let's look at its origins. Because the clouds of time have obscured so much, perhaps a starting place would be to dispel at least one theory of the spud's beginnings. It is, in fact, the only theory that can safely be eliminated. Those who say the potato first appeared in the colony of Virginia in the United States have been proved almost conclusively incorrect. Historians can prove the colonial settlement knew nothing at all of the potato at the time it was being grown in Europe. Indeed, one Russian scientist states the potato was unknown in colonial Virginia until as late as the 18th century.

Generally speaking, most researchers agree the potato first came to light in South America and it is here that the controversy begins. Some claim Chile as its birthplace, others say it's Peru and still others point to Colombia. It is at this point that archaeologists step in with a helping hand. Artifacts uncovered high in the mysterious Andes mountains feature the potato as the central image in some remarkable ceramic mugs, pots, and other vessels. Using carbon techniques, archaeologists have fixed the date of the pottery as having been cast in the second century, far earlier than anything else relating to the potato. Ancient though they may be, these historic finds are some of the finest examples of ceramic art in the world. Based on these findings it is probable that South American Indians living in the Andes region of Peru were the first to cultivate the plant.

The first white man to see the potato most probably was one of the Spanish Conquistadores. The Spaniards, under Pizarro, invaded Peru in 1535 and records reveal they found the plant being cultivated at that time by the Incas. In 1537 one of the invaders, Gonzalo de Quesada, wrote that the natives were eating 'truffles', a description of which perfectly matches the potato. Some historians however hold that the potato was first uncovered in the South American region of Colombia by Cieza de Leon in 1538. On the other hand, Russian research into the potato points to the plant's birthplace as Chile. These are just some of the numerous claims and counter-claims, but at least we have established the potato's origins as South American.

But getting the vegetable from South America to Europe remains yet another heavily-clouded issue, although most certainly it arrived on the European scene in the 16th century. One view holds that the Spanish returned with it on their ships and it was planted and used for food as early as 1576. It is also claimed that the potato plant was being grown in Italian gardens by the year 1588, not as a food but as a decorative plant. The potato's introduction to European shores, others say, was the result of Sir Francis Drake's voyage to South America. History records the English explorer first met up with the potato in Chile in 1579. But Drake did not return to England until 1580. If he did take the potato on board the seed tubers would not have survived the long journey home.

But who brought it to Ireland? Again, there is a lack of concrete evidence as to who that individual was or even the precise year it reached Ireland's green shores. Once more, conflicting claims persist.

Popular legend gives credit to Sir Walter Raleigh but historians debunk the theory that he planted the first crop in Ireland on his return from the Colony of Virginia in 1623, on the incontrovertible evidence, that Raleigh was dead by then! Another legend has it that Drake gave the tubers to Raleigh who planted them in Youghal. Asking his gardener for a dish of the new plant he was presented with a plate of the bitter berries, whereupon he ordered his gardener to root them up; neither Raleigh nor his gardener realising that it was the tuber and not the berry that was eaten.

There is also speculation that the potato arrived here by accident. When a fierce storm wrecked the Spanish ships of the Great Armada in 1588 many foundered on the west coast of Ireland. These ships which may have carried potatoes as cargo of foodstuffs, were plundered and the potato could have been introduced to Ireland in this way.

But by accident or design, the potato did arrive here and was a major crop by 1610. It quickly became the prime food in the lives of nearly half the nation and resulted in the almost exclusive association of the potato with Ireland, an association which continues even today.

The climate and soil in Ireland were particularly favourable to the growth of potatoes while the political and attendant economic instability of the country made the cultivation of a convenient food crop that required little land to produce good yields, and one that could be grown for most of the year, a necessity. In the seventeenth century it proved the salvation of the people when the corn failed for two years running during Cromwell's war. By the nineteenth century the dependence on the potato was complete. It has been estimated that the average peasant consumed ten pounds of spuds a day when they were available. In 1845, of a population of eight million, more than five million depended entirely on potatoes to survive.

In 1842 potato crops in eastern United States and Canada began to falter. In August of 1845 the blight hit Europe and the following month appeared in Ireland, in County Waterford and County Wexford. No one at the time could have imagined the ramifications. With no warning blossoming potato plants were reduced to withering thin black stalks in less than a day and before the potatoes could be pulled from the ground they sprouted black spots which swiftly turned the entire tuber into a black ball of rot. Their stench was sickening. The blight was severe and spread wildly and by the following summer the devastation was complete throughout the land. Approximately one million Irish perished from hunger and related diseases, including the so-called famine fever, a form of typhus. Dysentery and scurvy also took their toll and yet another million Irish fled the country, heading for Canada and the United States.

AN HONOURED PLACE

Although it carries both blessing and curses for its role in social history, the potato most certainly enjoys an honoured place in such diverse fields as literature, art, medicine and industry.

In literature the praise of the potato knows no bounds. The venerable bard, William Shakespeare, might have had a great hunger on him when he had Falstaff in *The Merry Wives of Windsor* proclaim: "Let

the sky rain potatoes; Let it thunder to the tune of
'Green Sleeves'." The potato also captured the imagi-
nation of Elizabeth Barrett Browning who, concerned
with the future of its cultivation, posed the question
in her poem *Aurora Leigh*: 'And is the potato to
become extinct like the moly?' (The moly is the plant
with black roots and white flowers which was given to
Ulysses by Hermes to counteract the evil spells of the
witch Circe.) The novelist Joseph Conrad went so far
as to give the tuber a prominent role in his story 'A
Smile of Fortune'. And the spud is the only veggie I
know that has its own book of poetry. Entitled *An
Anthology of the Potato* it was published in Dublin in
1961. The collection was garnered not only from
Ireland but from the United States, England and
Scotland as well.

The humble spud catapults into a position of
prominence in, of all places, the field of medicine
where its powers extend to many diseases. Just as the
historical background of the potato is clouded by the
passage of time, so too are the origins of many of the
miracle 'cures' attributed to it. The potato was once
hailed as a cure for leprosy. And sure enough there
was a counter-claim that the potato not only didn't
cure leprosy but indeed was the cause of the dreaded
illness. Tuberculosis and rickets were supposed to
vanish merely by eating the cooked vegetable and
indigestion disappear as soon as the sufferer chewed
a slice of the raw potato. Those suffering from tooth-
ache were promised a quick cure if they carried a
peeled potato around in the pocket.

'Apples of Love' was the title given to the potato
from numerous quarters because of its supposed
aphrodisiac qualities. So widespread was this belief it
was thought that the population explosion in Ireland
in the nineteenth century was attributable to the
potato. Lord Byron alluded to the aphrodisiacal
powers of the potato in Canto XV of his epic *Don Juan*

where he refers to the 'sad result of passions and potatoes'.

To achieve the desired state, one first had to boil or bake the tubers, then peel them and dip them in sugar and orange juice before eating. Alas, it was also discovered that flatulence was a by-product of the mixture.

The potato's popularity spread like wildfire after its introduction into Europe. What other veggie can you think of that was so exalted its blossom was once used to decorate m'lady's hair? Marie Antoinette thought none the less of its beauty.

Ah, but the esteem of the potato doesn't end there. It should not be overlooked that at one time the Swiss army had a marching song which saluted the spud in 'Chanson des Pommes de Terre'.

In the world of art no less a luminary than Vincent van Gogh was captivated by the potato. He devoted at least four still-life paintings to the subject. Some say his greatest work is a painting entitled 'The Potato Eaters'. It was completed in 1885 and depicts a peasant family sitting down to a meal of potatoes after a tiring day's work.

In industry too the potato has proved its worth. Potato starch is preferred for sizing and coating in the paper and textile industries. Dextrose used in the preparation of pharmaceutical products and commercial glucose used in tanning also depends on the potato. While alcohol (most notably in Poland and West Germany) can be produced by the fermentation of cooked potatoes by yeast.

OLD-FASHIONED REMEDIES

In Ireland the versatile potato has traditionally had a variety of non-cooking uses, mostly associated with the curing of different sorts of ailments. Indeed, in various parts of the country today it is not uncommon to meet someone who remembers their mother using the potato to help cure a case of badly infected tonsils. A sore throat called for the same treatment. In such cases, the remedy called for the stuffing of hot (really hot) boiled potatoes into a woollen stocking which was then wrapped around the neck and left overnight. The next day's dawn invariably saw the patient fully recovered.

A dried potato worn around the neck was a sure cure for rheumatism. Another version of this advises the sufferer to steal a potato and carry it around in the pocket. Never mind that it will shrivel and become squashy. Eventually the process will reverse itself and the spud will harden to the consistency of a stone, taking away the rheumatic aches and pains. Devotees of this version claimed the spud hardened as a result of absorbing the acid salts caused by the disease.

A badly infected finger, hand, toe or foot also required assistance from the spud. In such cases a poultice was made with various herbs and mixed with the water from a pot of boiled potatoes. A simpler method was merely to soak the affected part in the hot potato water. Relief, it was claimed, was often speedy and complete.

Body warts also fell before the potato treatment. The patient simply sliced a potato in half and rubbed the wart with the surface of the raw potato for three or four consecutive days. The wart would gradually grow smaller and eventually fall off.

Ingrown foot warts required a slightly different treatment. Here one would boil a potato, mash it up and add to it a teaspoonful of castor oil. The mixture was applied liberally on the painful area and the patient then covered it with a woollen stocking and wore it to bed. This process would be repeated every night for a week and at the end of seven days the foot would be free from the irritable wart.

The potato is, and always has been, many things to many people and it has as many names as there are places where it grows. The Incas called them papas. To the French they are pommes de terre, while in Spain they are papata. They are kartofel to a German and the Irish call them Murphys, spuds or praties. But by whatever name you choose to call them, the world's affair with the potato continues to flourish and when you too have discovered their enormous versatility as displayed in the recipes on the following pages, you won't be surprised.

SOUPS, STEWS AND CHOWDERS

from Ode to a Pratie

Thy name is Murphy. On the Antrim hills
There's cruffles and white-rocks; there's skerries, too, and dukes,
And kidneys – which is early; and champions and flukes –
Which doesn't help the farmer much to pay his bills:
The sort's not recommended. Then there's early rose,
And forty-folds, and flounders – which is bad;
And magnum bonums: – if good seed's to be had
It is the biggest pratie that the country grows,
And taste's not bad. Some grows best in rigs
And some in drills. There's sorts ye cudn't ate;
There's others dry and floury that's a trate;
And weeshy kinds, that's only fit for pigs.
Some likes a sandy sile and some a turfy,
Others do their best in good stiff clay:
There's new varieties appearin' iv'ry day;
But, as I said, thy fam'ly name is Murphy.

John Stevenson

Potato Cucumber Soup

5 medium potatoes, peeled and thinly sliced
1 small onion, peeled and sliced
8 ozs. (227 gm) cucumber, peeled and thinly sliced
1 teaspoon parsley
½ teaspoon mixed herbs
4 fl. ozs. (114 ml) milk
4 fl. ozs. (114 ml) cream
1 tablespoon butter
salt, black pepper and sugar to taste

In a three-quart saucepan cook the potatoes, onion and cucumber in enough water to cover the vegetables. When tender, drain off the water. Mash the vegetables. Add the milk, cream, herbs, butter and spices. Heat before serving. Sprinkle each bowl with a dash of paprika. Serves 4. For potato soup just omit the cucumber. Serve hot or cold.

Potato and Cabbage Soup

4 large potatoes, peeled and sliced
1 lb. (454 gm) diced raw cabbage
4 ozs. (114 gm) chopped onion
1 oz. (28 gm) butter
1 pint (568 ml) water
½ teaspoon black pepper
8 fl. ozs. (227 ml) cream

In a large pot cook onion slowly in butter until golden brown. Add water, pepper, potatoes and cabbage. Cook until tender. Add cream. Stir while reheating. Serve with toasted bread cubes and a dash of paprika. Serves 6.

Potato Bisque

6 potatoes, peeled and chopped
4 ozs. (114 gm) chopped onions
1 tablespoon parsley (fresh or dried)
½ teaspoon black pepper
½ teaspoon paprika
2 stalks of celery, sliced
1 tablespoon sugar
1 pint (568 ml) water
1 oz. (28 ml) butter
1 pint (568 ml) milk
1 oz. (28 gm) flour
2 eggs, beaten

Combine potatoes, onions, parsley, celery and water.
Cook in a large pot until tender. Mash well. Make a
white sauce with butter, flour and milk in a small
saucepan. Add to the cooked, mashed vegetables and
heat. Add the eggs, sugar, black pepper and paprika.
Heat again. Serves 6.

Quick Cheese Soup

8 ozs. (227 gm) cooked, mashed potatoes
1 bouillon cube
14 fl. ozs. (398 ml) boiling water
1 lb. (454 gm) grated, sharp cheddar cheese
16 fl. ozs. (455 ml) tomato juice
8 ozs. (227 gm) toasted bread cubes

For all cheese lovers this is a delicious and easy soup
to make. In a medium size saucepan, dissolve bouillon in boiling water. Blend in the mashed potato and
mix well. Add the tomato juice and cheese to the

bouillon-potato mixture. Simmer and stir well until the cheese is melted and the soup is hot. Garnish with toasted bread cubes. Serves 4.

Druids Lamb and Potato Stew

4 large potatoes, peeled and cubed
1½ lbs. (681 gm) boneless lamb, cut in one inch cubes
½ fl. oz. (14 ml) oil or fat
1 oz. (28 gm) flour
½ teaspoon black pepper
1 teaspoon garlic salt
4 fl. oz. (114 ml) white wine
1 teaspoon caraway seeds
8 small carrots, peeled and sliced
6 small onions, peeled

Brown lamb in oil in a large pot. When browned sprinkle with flour, pepper and garlic salt. Stir well to coat meat. Add the wine, the caraway seeds and just enough water to cover the meat. Cover the pot and simmer for 1 hour. Add the vegetables, cover with water. Then return the lid to the pot and simmer until vegetables are tender. This recipe makes 4 to 5 servings.

Oyster Festival Stew

5 medium potatoes, peeled and diced
12 ozs. (340 gm) raw shelled oysters with juice
1 small onion, peeled and diced
2 ozs. (57 ml) butter
1 pint (568 ml) milk
10 fl. ozs. (284 ml) cream
½ teaspoon salt
½ teaspoon black pepper
1 tablespoon parsley
1 tablespoon sugar

This potato-based recipe, using oysters, evokes memories of Galway's annual oyster festival.

Boil potatoes in water until tender. Drain and set aside. Heat butter in a large pan and fry onions until golden brown. Add oysters and juice, stir until hot then add potatoes, milk, cream, salt, pepper, parsley and sugar. Heat again. Thicken with a little flour and cold water mixed together if desired. Reheat at serving time. Good with crackers or bread. Serves 4.

Best Beef Stew

8 potatoes, peeled and cubed
2 lbs. (908 gm) lean beef, cubed
2 beef bouillon cubes
½ teaspoon black pepper
1 teaspoon chopped parsley
½ teaspoon basil or rosemary
1 large onion, chopped
6 carrots, peeled and cubed
4 ozs. (114 gm) flour
6 fl. ozs. (170 ml) cold water

In a large covered pot boil 2 litres of water. Dissolve bouillon cubes and set aside. In a frying-pan brown the cubed beef, onions and herbs in a little butter. When done, add this to the bouillon broth. Simmer for 2 hours. Lastly, add the potatoes and carrots and cook until tender. Mix flour and cold water into a thin paste, add to boiling stew to thicken, stirring well. Delicious with hot buttered rolls or dumplings. Makes 6 servings.

The three most delightful things to see:
a garden of white potatoes covered in blossom,
a ship under sail and a woman giving birth.

Irish Saying.

Captain's Chowder

5 medium potatoes, peeled and sliced thinly
1½ lbs. (681 gm) cod or haddock
4 rashers of bacon, chopped
1 medium size onion, chopped
1 pint (568 ml) milk
8 fl. ozs (227 ml) cream
4 fl. ozs. (114 ml) white wine
salt, black pepper and parsley to flavour

Cover fish with water in a large pot. Simmer slowly for 10 minutes. Then remove any skin or bones and set fish flesh aside. Save broth for later use. Fry bacon rashers and set aside. Fry onion in bacon fat, then add potatoes and fish broth. Simmer for 10 minutes, or until potatoes are cooked. Add fish, milk, cream, wine and seasoning. Sprinkle fried, chopped bacon on top. Serve hot with cream crackers. This delicious chowder serves 4.

A woman told me that a woman told her
that she saw a woman who saw a woman
who made ale of potatoes.

Irish Saying.

Lighthouse Chowder

6 potatoes, peeled and chopped
5 rashers of bacon, chopped
1 onion, chopped
1 pint (568 ml) water
1 lb. (454 gm) fish fillets, chopped
10 ozs. (280 gm) cooked shrimp or prawns, shelled and rinsed
1 pint (568 ml) warm milk
1 oz. (28 ml) butter
1 tablespoon chives or green onion tops, chopped
salt and pepper to taste

This recipe is good and hearty and you can use different types of fish or shellfish.

Fry bacon and onion until golden brown. Place in a large pot with the potatoes, water, salt, pepper and fish. Cover and simmer until the potatoes are tender. Add warm milk, butter and chives. Reheat. This recipe makes 4 or 5 bowls. Serve with a basket of cream crackers or rolls and butter. Delicious!

Cody's Chowder

4 large potatoes, peeled and diced
2 - 14 oz. (397 gm) each tins of corn
1 onion, chopped
6 rashers of bacon, chopped
1½ pints (852 ml) milk
½ pint (284 ml) cream
1 tablespoon butter
1 teaspoon dried parsley
salt and pepper to taste

Fry bacon rashers in a large pot until crispy and brown. Add tinned corn, onion, potatoes, parsley, salt and pepper. Add ½ pint of water and boil slowly until potatoes are tender. Then add the milk, cream, butter and parsley and reheat. Makes 6 servings.

Sausage, Bean and Potato Chowder

8 ozs. (227 gm) peeled, diced potatoes
1 lb. (454 gm) bulk sausage meat
12 oz. (340 gm) tin of beans
14 oz. (397 gm) tin of tomatoes
4 fl. ozs. (114 ml) water
4 fl. ozs. (114 ml) red wine
½ teaspoon minced garlic
½ teaspoon onion salt
½ teaspoon black pepper
4 ozs. (114 gm) diced green peppers

Fry sausage meat in a large pot. When cooked, drain off the fat and add all the other ingredients. Cover.

Bring to the boil, then simmer for half an hour. Makes 4 to 6 helpings. Sprinkle the top with grated cheese if desired and serve with warm French bread.

Boluisce Chowder

8 potatoes, peeled and diced
4 ozs. (114 gm) chopped onions
2 ozs. (57 ml) butter
4 lbs. (1.82 kg) white fish fillets, skinned and cut into chunks
8 ozs. (227 gm) clams or mussels, shelled and chopped
8 ozs. (227 gm) scallops, shelled and cut into quarters
8 ozs. (227 gm) shrimp or prawns, shells removed
2 - 14½ oz. (410 ml each) tins of evaporated milk
salt and pepper to taste

John Glanville, proprietor of the Boluisce Seafood Bar, Spiddal, County Galway, serves this hearty, delicious chowder. A visit to his cosy pub restaurant with the cheery turf fire glowing is a flavourful must for those passing along the Connemara shore road.

Fry onion in butter in a large pot. Add fish fillets, clams, scallops and shrimp. Cover with water and simmer until tender. Add 2 tins of evaporated milk and diced potatoes. Cook until the potatoes are tender. Add salt and pepper. Serve hot with a dash of paprika to each serving. Good served with salted crackers. Makes 8 to 10 servings.

from Buttermilk and Praties

You may talk about your suppers grand,
   Of dishes covered with spices,
Your turkeys, oysters and fine meats
   And puddings, tarts and ices.
But better than them all combined
   The Irishman's great trate is –
Taste it once, you'll surely find,
   'Tis buttermilk and praties.
      Tu ral tu, tu ral tu –

I've dined with great epicures
   Many a time and a place sirs;
I've wint pig's-fry till, by me soul,
   A snout grew on my face sirs!
Though pig's head and cabbage is very good,
   but devil a meal so swate is,
As a noggin of fresh buttermilk;
   With a skillet of floury praties.
      Tu ral tu, tu ral tu –

An Irishman no one can stand
   When armed with a shillelah;
He'll fight till death does stop his breath,
   And after that I'll bail ye:
And that what gives him courage true,
   That shapes him clane and nate is,
Take my word, tis nothin else
   but buttermilk and praties.
      Tu ral tu, tu ral tu –

Nineteenth century ballad

SALADS

The Praties They are Small

Oh! the Praties they are small over here – over here
Oh! the Praties they are small over here,
Oh! the Praties they are small, and we dug them in the fall,
And we ate them skins and all, full of fear – full of fear.

Oh! I wish that we were geese in the morn – in the morn,
Oh! I wish that we were geese in the morn,
Oh! I wish that we were geese, for they live and die in peace,
Till the hour of their decease, eatin corn – eatin corn.

Oh! we're down into the dust, over here – over here
Oh, we're down into the dust over here,
Oh! we're down into the dust, but the Lord in whom we trust,
Will soon give us crumb or crust over here – over here.

Traditional Song.

Hot Potato Salad

6 medium sized peeled, cooked potatoes
6 rashers of bacon, chopped
4 ozs. (114 gm) chopped peeled onions
1 oz. (28 gm) flour
2 ozs. (57 gm) sugar
½ teaspoon celery salt or celery seed
½ teaspoon black pepper
4 fl. ozs. (114 ml) warm water
2 fl. ozs. (57 ml) vinegar

This versatile salad can be served with any number of side dishes.

Cut hot cooked potatoes into chunks, keep warm. Fry the bacon and onion. Remove when cooked and add to the potatoes. Keep warm. Heat the bacon fat in the skillet, add flour, stirring well. Add water, vinegar, celery salt or seed, pepper and sugar. Pour this mixture over the hot potatoes, bacon and onion. Mix lightly and serve hot. Makes 6 servings.

Potato Salad with Yogurt

3 lbs. (1.36 kg) peeled, cooked, cold, diced potatoes
4 ozs. (114 gm) diced onion with green tops or scallions
4 ozs. (114 gm) diced celery
4 hard boiled eggs, peeled and chopped
8 ozs. (227 gm) mayonnaise
8 ozs. (227 gm) yogurt
1 teaspoon hot English mustard
1 teaspoon horseradish sauce
1 teaspoon celery salt
4 ozs. (114 gm) diced cucumber

The yogurt gives this delicious recipe a nice tangy flavour.

Mix all the ingredients in a large salad bowl and chill well until serving time. For a party dish you can garnish this salad with parsley, green pepper rings, olives or paprika. Serves 8.

Hot Sauerkraut Potato Salad

4 potatoes, peeled, cooked and sliced
2 ozs. (57 gm) butter
6 sausages, sliced
1 small onion, chopped
2 ozs. (57 gm) brown sugar
1½ lbs. (681 gm) sauerkraut
2 eggs, beaten

This salad is a meal in itself.

In a large frying pan heat the butter. Add sausage and onion and fry until lightly browned. Drain sauerkraut juice into the frying pan. Add sugar and bring to the boil. Add eggs and heat again. Stir well. Combine the sauerkraut, potatoes and a dash of pepper in a large casserole or baking dish. Pour in the sausage, onion and egg mixture. Bake uncovered in a hot oven for 20 to 25 minutes, (180°C/350°F/gas 5). Serves 6.

Swiss Cheese and Potato Salad

6 medium size peeled, cooked potatoes
16 ozs. (454 gm) Swiss cheese
2 oz. (57 gm) onion
1 teaspoon celery salt
1 teaspoon black pepper
8 ozs. (227 gm) mayonnaise

Chop cheese, potatoes and onion. Add the other ingredients and mix well. Chill and trim with anchovy fillets. Serves 8.

Skipper Salad

1 lb. (454 gm) potatoes, peeled, cooked and diced (cold)
1 tin kippered herrings
1 medium red onion, sliced into rings
4 hard boiled eggs, peeled and chopped
salad dressing:
2 ozs. (57 ml) tomato ketchup, 4 ozs. (114 ml) mayonnaise,
  tablespoon sugar

This salad goes well with herring. Smoked haddock or smoked mackeral also make a good combination.

Mix the ketchup, mayonnaise and sugar together. Set

aside. Remove skin and bone from the herring. In a medium size bowl mix fish, potatoes, onion rings and the eggs. Mix in the salad dressing. Serve on lettuce. Makes 4 servings.

Supper Salad

8 ozs. (227 gm) diced, cooked peeled potatoes
8 medium size fresh tomatoes
1 hard boiled egg, peeled and chopped
½ teaspoon celery salt
1 teaspoon sugar
½ teaspoon mustard
2 ozs. (57 ml) mayonnaise

Wash and dry each tomato. Remove a small slice from the top of each tomato and carefully scoop out the inside. Set the empty tomatoes aside. Chop the pulp and place in a medium sized bowl. Mix in all the other ingredients and fill the empty tomatoes with this mixture. Sprinkle with paprika. Serve on lettuce. 4 servings at 2 tomatoes per person.

Round Tower Salad

2 lbs. (908 gm) chopped, cooked potatoes
1½ lbs. (681 gm) chilled, chopped corned beef
*   (tinned or fresh)*
8 ozs. (227 gm) chopped celery
4 ozs. (114 gm) peeled minced onion
12 ozs. (340 gm) chopped, unpeeled apples
4 ozs. (114 gm) chopped, peeled cucumber
3 hard boiled eggs, peeled and sliced
salad dressing:
2 fl. ozs. (57 ml) vinegar, 2 fl. ozs. (57 ml) salad oil,
1 teaspoon mustard, 1 teaspoon sugar

This salad reminds me of family picnics long ago. It was always served to us with cooling glasses of lemonade. The grown-ups, I've come to suspect, enjoyed beverages of another sort!

Using a large bowl, combine beef, potatoes, celery, onion, apples, cucumber, and eggs. Chill well. At serving time prepare the salad dressing. Pour over the salad and mix. Serve on lettuce. Delicious with rolls and butter. Makes 6 servings.

Hot Limerick Ham Salad

1½ lbs. (681 gm) cooked potatoes, diced
2 ozs. (57 gm) chopped green pepper
2 ozs. (57 gm) chopped onion
1 lb. (454 gm) chopped ham
½ fl. oz. (14 ml) cooking oil
4 ozs. (114 ml) mayonnaise
10 ozs. (280 gm) cheddar cheese, grated

Fry onions, green pepper and ham in oil in a large pan

until golden brown in colour. Add potatoes and mayonnaise, and reheat. Stir in the grated cheddar cheese and heat just enough to melt the cheese. Season to taste. Serve hot. Makes 6 servings.

Love of my heart the potatoes
That need not kiln nor mill
But their digging in the garden
And their laying on the fire.

Irish Saying.

Galway Fish and Potato Salad

1 lb. (454 gm) cooked potatoes, chilled and diced
1 lb. (454 gm) cold, cooked white fish, shredded
2 ozs. (57 gm) green onion tops, chopped
½ teaspoon paprika
1 teaspoon celery salt
8 ozs. (227 ml) mayonnaise or salad cream
½ teaspoon black pepper

Serve this salad with sweet pickles, fruit chutney and hot tea.

Combine all ingredients, mix and chill well. Garnish with hard boiled egg slices and parsley. Makes 8 servings.

OVEN-BAKED DISHES

The Potato Digger's Song

Come, Connal, acushla, turn the clay,
    And show the lumpers the light, gossoon;
For we must toil this autumn day,
    With heaven's help till the rise of the moon.
Our corn is stocked, our hay secure,
    Thank God! and nothing my boy remains,
But to pile the potatoes safe on the floor
    Before the coming November rains,
The peasant's mine is his harvest still;
  So now, my lad, let's dig with a will:-
   Work hand and foot,
    Work spade and hand,
    Work spade and hand,
     Through the crumbly mould;
     The blessed fruit
      That grows at the root
      Is the real gold
      Of Ireland!

Thomas Caulfield Irwin

Malin Head Hash

12 ozs. (340 gm) chopped cooked potatoes
12 ozs. (340 gm) chopped cooked corned beef
4 ozs. (114 gm) chopped onion
1 teaspoon minced parsley
2 tablespoons Worcestershire sauce
1 teaspoon black pepper
1 - 6 fl. ozs. (170 ml) tin evaporated milk
4 ozs. (114 gm) crushed cornflakes
2 tablespoons melted butter
Make 4 poached eggs at serving time

This corned-beef hash is delicious and with the poached eggs on top at serving time this dish is a hearty full meal.

Lightly mix the corned-beef, potatoes, onion, parsley, pepper, evaporated milk and Worcestershire sauce. Turn into a greased baking dish. Mix the cornflakes and melted butter. Sprinkle on top. Bake in oven for 30 minutes (180°C/350°F/gas 4). Serve each portion with an egg on top. Delicious with tomato ketchup or fruit chutney. Makes 4 servings.

Potato Stuffed Haddock

3 potatoes, peeled and boiled
2 onions, peeled and boiled
2 ozs. (57 ml) soft butter
½ teaspoon salt
¼ teaspoon black pepper
1 teaspoon mixed herbs
1 - 2/3 lb. (908 gm) haddock, gutted

Finely chop potatoes and onions together. Add soft

butter, salt, pepper and herbs to potato-onion mix, stirring well. Wash and dry fish. Fill with stuffing and sew together. Brush fish with butter. Place in an oiled baking pan and bake in oven for 40 to 50 minutes, (180°C/350° F/gas 4). Serves 4 to 6 depending on size of the fish.

Tasty Potato Torte

6 potatoes
3 ozs. (85 ml) butter
4 ozs. (114 gm) grated Parmesan cheese
½ teaspoon nutmeg
½ teaspoon salt
¼ teaspoon black pepper
4 ozs. (114 gm) grated Swiss cheese
3 fl. ozs. (85 ml) cream
2 ozs. (57 gm) chopped green onion tops or chives

This recipe is perfect for brunch or tea. It is very much like a quiche but without the bother. Delicious with green salad.

Butter a large ovenproof casserole dish. Thinly slice peeled potatoes. Layer the casserole dish, using potatoes, Parmesan cheese, nutmeg, salt and pepper. Cover and bake in oven for 1 hour (180°C/350°F/gas 4). Remove from oven. Pour cream over potatoes. Sprinkle grated Swiss cheese and green onions on top. Place under grill for a few minutes to brown. Remove from grill. Serve hot. Makes 4 servings.

Tuna Crisp Casserole

2 packets potato crips
7 ozs. (199 gm) can tuna fish (drained)
10 oz. (295 gm) tin condensed cream of mushroom soup
4 ozs. (114 gm) grated cheese
1 tablespoon minced onion

When time is short this dish is quick and easy·

Mix tuna fish, mushroom soup, cheese and onion. Pour into a buttered baking dish. Crush potato crisps and sprinkle over top. Bake in oven for 25 to 30 minutes (180°C/350°F/gas 4). Delicious served with a green salad or cole-slaw. Makes 4 servings.

Salmon Birds' Nests

20 ozs. (568 gm) cooked mashed potato
1 oz. (28 ml) butter
1 oz. (28 gm) minced onion
1 oz. (28 gm) chopped green onion
1 oz. (28 gm) diced green pepper
10 oz. (295 gm) tin condensed tomato soup
1 teaspoon mustard
1 teaspoon sugar
16 oz. (454 gm) tin salmon (remove bones)
4 ozs. (114 gm) dry breadcrumbs
2 ozs. (57 ml) melted butter for breadcrumb topping

An old Irish tale has it that the legendary Finn MacCool once stuck his finger into a cooking salmon and got burnt. After that, whenever he sucked his finger he was blessed with supernatural knowledge. Now this salmon recipe carries no guarantee of bestowing such grand powers, but it will indeed make you feel like the fabled Finn himself.

Fry onion, onion tops, and green pepper in 1 oz. of butter. Add soup, mustard and sugar. Heat and add salmon. Keep this mixture warm. Grease a large baking tray. Shape mashed potato into 6 bird's nest shapes on the tray and fill each with salmon mixture. Mix breadcrumbs with 2 ozs. of melted butter. Top each nest with crumbs. Bake in oven for about 10 minutes (200g°C/400°F/gas 6). Serves 6.

Creamed Potato and Eggs

---

16 ozs. (454 gm) potatoes peeled, sliced and cooked
4 hard boiled eggs (peeled and sliced)
6 ozs. (171 gm) dry breadcrumbs
2 ozs. (57 ml) melted butter for breadcrumb topping
8 ozs. (227 gm) chopped cooked ham or chopped beef
White Sauce:
2 ozs. (57 ml) butter, 2 ozs. (57 gm) flour,
12 fl. ozs. (341 ml) milk

Just right for the budget-conscious cook and a good way to put left-overs to use.

Make white sauce: Melt 2 ozs. butter in a pan over medium heat. Add 2 ozs. flour to blend. While stirring add milk and mix until thickened. Add the chopped meat to the white sauce and keep warm. Butter a large baking dish. Mix the potatoes and eggs and place in the baking dish. Pour the white sauce over. Blend breadcrumbs with 2 ozs. melted butter and sprinkle on top of the casserole. Bake in oven for 30 minutes or until potatoes are tender (180°C/350°F/gas 4). Makes 4 servings.

Tinkers' Salmon Casserole

16 ozs. (454 gm) cooked mashed potatoes
1 (340 gm) large tin of salmon
4 eggs, beaten
4 ozs. (114 gm) grated Parmesan cheese
4 ozs. (114 gm) dry breadcrumbs
1 tablespoon lemon juice
2 ozs. (57 gm) flour
2 ozs. (57 ml) butter
12 fl. ozs. (341 ml) milk

This casserole is hearty and nutritious. The lemon juice brings out the flavour. You can use ¾ lb. fresh cooked salmon instead of the tinned salmon.

Prepare mashed potatoes and set aside. Remove bones and skin from the salmon. Set aside. Prepare a white sauce: Blend flour with butter over medium heat. Stir in the milk and bring to a slow boil until thickened. Set aside and keep warm. In a large bowl combine potatoes, salmon, eggs, cheese and lemon juice. Pour this mixture into a buttered ovenware baking dish and sprinkle with breadcrumbs. Bake in oven for 35 minutes until puffy (180°C/350°F/gas 4). Spoon white sauce over each serving. Serves 4.

Dublin Coddle

6 large potatoes, peeled and sliced
8 thick rashers of bacon (cut in half)
10 pork sausages (cut in half)
3 large onions, peeled and sliced
1 oz. (28 gm) chopped parsley
salt, pepper and sugar to taste

Dublin Coddle is an old favourite. Traditionally this dish was cooked in a large heavy pot set on a hot glowing turf fire. The pot was then covered and more heated sods placed all over and around the cooking vessel.

Cook sausages and rashers in boiling water for 20 minutes. Remove meat to a large casserole dish. Save the liquid. Make layers of meat, onion, potatoes, parsley, sugar, salt and pepper. Add reserved meat stock to about ¼ from the top of the casserole. Cover and bake in a slow oven for about 60 minutes (120°C/250°F/gas 2). Serves 6.

Potato and Cottage Cheese Pie

12 ozs. (340 gm) cooked mashed potatoes
9 inch unbaked pie pastry
10 ozs. (280 gms) cottage cheese
4 ozs. (114 ml) sour cream
2 eggs, beaten
1 teaspoon salt
½ teaspoon black pepper
4 ozs. (114 gm) sliced scallions or green onion tops
2 ozs. (57 gm) grated Parmesan cheese

Blend cottage cheese until smooth. Beat in mashed

potatoes, sour cream, eggs, salt, pepper and scallions. Pour into pie shell. Sprinkle Parmesan cheese over top. Bake in oven for 50 minutes until firm (180°C/350°F/gas 4). Serves 4 to 6.

To make sour cream mix 4 ozs. fresh cream, 1 oz. lemon juice. Stir to thicken.

Frosted Lamb and Potato Loaf

16 ozs. (454 gm) cooked mashed potatoes
2 lbs. (908 gm) minced lamb
4 ozs. (114 gm) minced onion
8 ozs. (227 gm) soft breadcrumbs
1 teaspoon mixed herbs
1 oz. (28 ml) tomato ketchup
1 egg, beaten
3 fl. ozs. (85 ml) cream
1 - 6 oz. (171 gm) jar apple sauce

Meat stays nice and juicy prepared in this way as the mashed potato covering keeps it moist.

In a large mixing bowl combine all the ingredients, except mashed potato and apple sauce. Form meat mixture into a loaf on a shallow baking pan. Bake in oven for 40 minutes (180°C/350°F/gas 4). Remove from oven. Spread mashed potato on top of meat. Return to oven for another 20 minutes. Arrange meat on a platter, garnish with apple sauce. Serve hot. Makes 6 to 8 servings.

Pork Chops – Irish Style

4 medium potatoes, peeled and thinly sliced
4 large thick pork chops
salt and pepper to taste
1 oz. (28 ml) vegetable oil
2 ozs. (57 gm) sliced onion
10 oz. (295 gm) tin condensed cream of mushroom soup
4 fl. ozs. (114 ml) milk
12 ozs. (340 gm) shredded cabbage

Season pork chops with salt and pepper. Brown chops on both sides in a hot greased pan for 15 minutes. Remove chops and set aside. Add cooking oil to pan. Fry onion until golden brown. Add mushroom soup and milk. Stir to heat. Grease a large baking dish. Make 2 layers using potatoes, cabbage and mushroom soup mixture in each layer. Top with pork chops and cover. Bake in oven for 1 hour (180°C/350°F/gas 4). Makes 4 servings.

Porcupine Pie

4 potatoes, peeled
1 lb. (454 gm) minced beef
4 ozs. (114 gm) uncooked rice
1 small onion chopped
¼ teaspoon mixed herbs
½ teaspoon salt
½ teaspoon pepper
10 oz. (295 gm) tin condensed tomato soup
5 fl. ozs. (142 ml) milk
5 fl. ozs. (142 ml) water

This is an unusual combination of rice and potato but a guaranteed delight.

Mix minced beef, uncooked rice, onion, herbs, salt and pepper into a large bowl. Shape into small meatballs. Place them in the bottom of a greased baking dish. Slice the raw potatoes thinly and place over meatballs. Mix tomato soup, water and milk. Pour over potatoes. Cover baking dish. Bake in oven for 45 minutes (180°C/350°F/gas 4). Makes 4 to 6 servings.

Potato and Mushroom Bake

12 ozs. (340 gm) cooked, sliced potatoes
12 sausages, cooked, sliced
4 oz. (114 gm) jar mushrooms, drained
4 hard boiled eggs
1 small onion, sliced
4 ozs. (114 gm) mild, grated cheese
4 ozs. (114 gm) dry breadcrumbs
2 ozs. (57 ml) melted butter
6 fl. ozs. (170 ml) white wine
1 oz. (28 gm) flour

The wine, cheese and mushrooms give this casserole an elegant flavour, yet it is quite simple to prepare.

Slice eggs, set aside. Fry onion and sausage in a large pan. Remove and slice sausages. Set aside. Add a little butter to fat in pan. When hot add flour. Add milk, stirring to thicken. Add white wine and continue to stir. In a large greased baking dish put eggs, potato, sausage, onion, mushrooms and cheese. Mix breadcrumbs with melted butter. Set aside. Pour sauce over casserole. Sprinkle buttered crumbs on top. Bake in oven for 30 minutes (180°C/350°F/gas 4). Makes 4 servings.

Connemara Surprise

6 large potatoes, peeled, boiled
2 ozs. (57 ml) melted butter
4 hard-boiled eggs, peeled, sliced
3½ oz. (99 gm) tin anchovy fillets
4 fl. ozs. (114 ml) cream
½ teaspoon black pepper
2 ozs. (57 ml) grated Parmesan cheese
4 ozs. (114 gm) grated cheddar cheese

Slice potatoes in large pieces. In a large, greased baking dish, make 3 layers – potatoes, egg slices, pepper, anchovies and grated cheeses. Pour cream over all and bake uncovered for 25 minutes (180°C/350°F/gas 4). Makes 4 servings.

Cassidy's Cakes

12 ozs. (340 gm) cooked, mashed potato
1 lb. (454 gm) smelts
2 ozs. (57 ml) soft butter
1 tablespoon lemon juice
1 tablespoon minced onion
½ teaspoon pepper
1 teaspoon sugar
4 fl. ozs. (114 ml) cream
8 ozs. (227 gm) breadcrumbs
3 oz. (85 gm) pkt. instant white sauce

This is a wholesome and economical dish. Spoon a little white sauce over each serving.

Boil smelts until bones and skin can be removed easily. Mash fish in a bowl, adding potato, butter, lemon juice, onion, pepper, sugar, and cream. Mix well. Shape this mixture into little cakes. Roll in the breadcrumbs, and place on a greased, shallow baking dish. Bake in oven for 25 minutes (180°C/350°F/gas 4). Serve with white sauce. Makes 4 servings.

Finnan Haddie with Potato Topping

12 ozs. (340 gm) cooked mashed potato
1½ lbs. (681 gm) finnan haddie (smoked haddock)
Enough milk to cover fish while boiling
4 ozs. (114 gm) grated cheddar cheese
8 fl. ozs. (227 ml) milk for sauce
2 ozs. (57 ml) butter
2 ozs. (57 gm) flour
1 green pepper, diced
4 ozs. (114 ml) cream

Place fish in a large greased baking dish. Cover fish with milk and bake in oven for 25 minutes (160°C/325°F/gas 3). When done, flake fish in the baking dish and set aside. Mix up mashed potato and cheese in a small dish and set aside. Make up the cream sauce in a small saucepan. Melt the butter, add the flour, milk, cream and the diced green pepper. Stir until thickened over low heat. Pour this sauce over fish in the baking dish. Top with cheese-potato mixture. Return casserole to the oven and bake for 25 minutes more at the same heat. Makes 4 to 6 servings.

Shamrock Tuna Pie

3 oz. (85 gm) pkt. instant mashed potato
2 eggs
4 fl. ozs. (114 ml) milk
10 ozs. (280 gm) soft breadcrumbs
1 teaspoon mustard
1 oz. (28 gm) parsley
4 ozs. (114 gm) minced onion
¼ teaspoon black pepper
2 - 7 oz. (199 gm each) tins tuna fish, drained
4 ozs. (114 gm) grated cheese

In a large mixing bowl blend eggs, milk, breadcrumbs, mustard, parsley, onion, pepper and tuna
fish. Pour mixture into a large, greased pie dish. Bake
in oven for 30 minutes (180°C/350°F/gas 4). Remove
from oven. Prepare mashed potato. Pile on top of tuna.
Sprinkle with cheese. Return to oven until hot and
cheese is melted. Serve with a green salad. 4 to 6
servings.

Fisherman's Delight

6 large potatoes
4 green peppers
4 medium onions
½ teaspoon minced garlic
4 ozs. (114 gm) grated Parmesan cheese
1 teaspoon paprika
½ teaspoon mixed herbs
4 ozs. (114 ml) vegetable oil

A hearty, substantial dish for a fisherman's appetite.
Serve with a man-sized sizzling steak.

Peel potatoes and cut into slices. Remove seeds from green peppers and cut into slices. Peel onions and slice into rings. Make layers of the vegetables in a large, greased casserole dish. Cover with cold water, add garlic, Parmesan cheese, paprika, herbs and oil. Stir and cover. Bake for 50 minutes in oven (180°C/350°F/gas 4). Serves 4 to 6.

Kate's Prawn Loaf

16 ozs. (454 gm) mashed potatoes
10 ozs. (280 gm) celery
1 small onion
1 green pepper
2 ozs. (57 ml) butter
12 ozs. (340 gm) prawns, cooked, shelled and diced
2 eggs, beaten
1 tablespoon chopped parsley
½ teaspoon black pepper

Made with either fresh or tinned shrimp or prawns, this is an easy-to-make meal.

Chop celery, onion and green pepper. Fry in butter until golden brown. In a large mixing bowl blend celery, onion, green pepper, prawns, beaten eggs, potatoes, pepper and parsley. Mix well. Pack this mixture into a greased loaf pan and bake in oven for 1 hour (180°C/350°F/gas 4). Delicious with white sauce and a green salad. Serves 6.

Kilroe Casserole

14 ozs. (397 gm) cooked mashed potatoes
1 lb. (454 gm) tinned salmon
3 eggs, beaten
4 oz. (114 gm) tin of mushrooms, drained
1 oz. (28 gm) chopped chives or scallions
½ teaspoon black pepper
2 medium tomatoes
6 ozs. (171 gm) grated sharp cheese
1 oz. (28 gm) chopped parsley
Combine: 4 ozs. (114 gm) dry breadcrumbs and
4 ozs. (114 gm) grated Parmesan cheese

Drain salmon. Remove bones. In a large bowl combine salmon, eggs, mushrooms, chives and pepper. Pour this mixture into a large buttered caserole. Cut tomatoes into slices and arrange on top of salmon mixture. Sprinkle with grated sharp cheese. Mix parsley with the prepared mashed potatoes. Spread on top of the salmon-tomato-cheese mixture in the casserole. Lastly, sprinkle with the bread-crumbs Parmesan cheese mix. Bake in oven for 30 to 35 minutes (180°C/350°F/gas 4). Makes 6 servings.

Salmon and Potato Pie

14 ozs. (397 gm) cooked mashed potatoes
4 ozs. (114 gm) chopped onion
1 oz. (28 ml) butter
14 oz. (397 gm) salmon cooked. Remove skin and bones.
1 tablespoon chopped chives
Pastry for 2 crust pie (9 inch pie plate)

All you need to make this a complete meal is an accompanying vegetable or in summer a salad.

Prepare pie crust and set aside. Prepare mashed potato, set aside. Fry onion in butter until golden brown. Add potato, salmon and chives. Mix well. Line bottom of pie plate with ½ pie pastry. Pour in salmon mixture for the filling. Place the other half of the pie pastry on top. Seal edges, make a few vents for steam to escape. Bake in oven for 45 minutes (200°C/400°F/gas 6). Makes 5 to 6 servings.

Betty's Ham & Potato Savoury

1½ lbs. (681 gm) cooked diced potatoes
3 ozs. (85 ml) butter
3 ozs. (85 gm) flour
16 fl. ozs. (455 ml) milk
8 ozs. (227 gm) grated sharp cheese
1 tablespoon prepared mustard
1 lb. (454 gm) sliced ham
Mix together:
4 ozs. (114 gm) dry breadcrumbs
1 oz. (28 ml) melted butter

Put your leftover ham to good use with this recipe.

Cook and dice potatoes. Set aside. Add flour to melted butter in a large pan over medium heat. Add milk slowly, stirring until white sauce thickens. Add mustard and grated cheese, stirring until cheese melts. Butter a large ovenware casserole. Make several layers using the potatoes, ham and cheese sauce. Sprinkle the buttered crumbs on top. Bake in oven for 30 to 40 minutes (180°C/350°F/gas 4). Makes 6 servings.

Shepherd's Pie

6 medium potatoes
4 fl. ozs. (114 ml) cream
1 teaspoon pepper
2 ozs. (57 ml) butter
1 large onion, peeled and diced
1 oz. (28 gm) flour
8 fl. ozs. (227 ml) boiling water
1 bouillon cube
16 ozs. (454 gm) cooked lamb, ground or chopped finely
3 tomatoes, sliced
1 teaspoon mixed herbs

Shepherd's Pie wouldn't *be* Shepherd's Pie without potatoes. This standard dish is tasty and economical.

Dissolve bouillon cube in boiling water. Set aside. Peel and cook potatoes. When tender drain and mash with milk and pepper until light and fluffy. Set aside. Melt butter in a pan. Fry onion until golden brown, then add 1 oz. flour and bouillon, stirring until mixture thickens. Add cooked lamb, sliced tomatoes and herbs. Heat again. Spread the meat mixture into a large buttered casserole. Spread the mashed potato over the meat. Bake in oven for 35 to 40 minutes (180°C/350°F/gas 4). Makes 4 servings.

Potato Crisps and Chicken

2 - 6 oz. (171 gm each) pkts. potato crisps (crushed)
4 chicken breasts (remove skin)
3 ozs. (85 ml) melted butter
1 - 1 oz. (28 gm) envelope cheese sauce mix
½ teaspoon garlic powder
½ teaspoon paprika
1 teaspoon dried parsley
½ teaspoon black pepper

Wash and dry chicken. Remove skin. Melt butter in a small pan. Mix crisps, dry cheese sauce mix, garlic powder, paprika, parsley and pepper in a small bowl. Oil a shallow ovenware tray. Dip chicken pieces in melted butter, then in the crisp mixture. Place on tray and bake in oven for 40 to 50 minutes (200°C/400°F/gas 6), or until done. Delicious hot or cold. Makes 4 servings.

Pub Pork Pie

3 ozs. (85 gm) instant mashed potato
1½ lbs. (681 gm) lean, boneless pork, diced
1 large onion, chopped
1 teaspoon rosemary
½ teaspoon black pepper
6 ozs. (171 gm) Ritz crackers or cream crackers, crushed
3 cooking apples, peeled and sliced
1 tablespoon sugar
1 fl. oz. (28 ml) lemon juice
2 ozs. (57 gm) flour
2 ozs. (57 ml) butter, melted

In a large bowl mix the pork with the onion, herbs, pepper and crushed crackers. In another bowl mix apples, sugar, lemon juice and flour. Grease a large ovenproof dish. Make layers of the pork mixture and the apple mixture. Cover and bake in oven for 1½ hours (180°C/350°C/gas 4). Make up mashed potato according to directions. Spread on top of the cooked pork and apple. Pour melted butter on top. Return to oven, uncovered. Allow to bake for a few minutes until potato crust is lightly browned. Makes 4 to 6 servings.

Potato and Chicken Pie

12 ozs. (340 gm) potatoes
1 - 5 lb. (2.27 kg) chicken
20 ozs. (568 ml) water
3 stalks celery, sliced
1 large onion, sliced
12 ozs. (340 gm) carrots
8 ozs. (227 gm) peas
1 bay leaf
2 - 10 oz. (295 gm each) tins cream of chicken soup
salt and pepper to taste

Wash and cut up chicken. Place in a large pot and cover with boiling water. Add celery, onions and bay leaf. Cook slowly until tender, 1 to 1½ hours. Remove chicken. When cool, remove meat from bones and set aside. Save the broth. Cook vegetables in a little water. Drain and set aside. In a large buttered baking dish place chopped chicken, cooked vegetables, salt and pepper. Heat cream of chicken soup in a saucepan, thinning it with some of the reserved chicken broth. Pour over chicken and vegetables. Cover and bake for 30 minutes (180°C/350°F/gas 4). You can put a pie crust on top before baking, or simply serve with hot rolls or toast. Makes 4 to 6 helpings.

Potato Burger

1½ lbs. (681 gm) minced beef
1 - 2 oz. (57 gm) pkt. instant brown gravy mix
1 - 10.4 oz. (295 gm) tin condensed cream of mushroom soup
8 fl. ozs. (227 ml) sour cream
4 fl. ozs. (114 ml) water
2 tablespoons tomato ketchup

For the Topping:
8 ozs. (227 gm) instant mashed potato flakes
8 ozs. (227 gm) flour
2 teaspoons baking powder
6 fl. ozs. (170 ml) milk
1 fl. oz. (28 ml) cooking oil
1 egg

A casserole like this is good eating and nutritious. You can feed 5 or 6 hungry people in a very economical manner.

Break meat into small pieces and place in a large ovenware casserole. Bake in oven for 25 minutes (200°C/400°F/gas 6). Remove from oven. Drain fat. Add gravy mix, soup, sour cream, water and ketchup to meat. Mix and set aside. Make the topping in another bowl. Mix flour, potato flakes, baking powder, milk, cooking oil and egg. Stir well. Drop by spoonfuls on top of meat. Return to oven for 30 minutes. Serve hot. Makes 5 to 6 servings.

To make Sour Cream Mix:
8 ozs. fresh cream, 2 ozs. lemon juice. Stir to thicken.

Quick Cheesy Potatoes

1 lb. pkt (454 gm) frozen chips or french fries
2 ozs. (57 ml) butter
6 ozs. (170 ml) cream
6 ozs. (171 gm) grated cheddar cheese
4 slices of processed cheese
1 teaspoon chopped chives
1 teaspoon onion salt
1 teaspoon black pepper

Short-cut tricks make a meal-in-a-minute and this tasty recipe never fails to appeal to young people.

In a saucepan heat together butter, cream, cheeses, chives, onion, salt and pepper. Stir until cheese is melted and sauce is smooth. Oil a large casserole and place chips or french fries in the bottom. Pour the cheese sauce over the potatoes. Stir and bake in oven for 45 to 50 minutes (180°C/350°F/gas 4). Makes 4 servings.

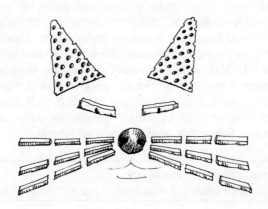

Kidneys with Potatoes and Mustard

12 ozs. (340 gm) mashed potato
6 beef kidneys
8 rashers of bacon
1 small onion, chopped
1 oz. (28 ml) butter
1 - 3 oz. (85 ml) tin mushrooms, drained
1 teaspoon paprika
1 teaspoon hot mustard
1 oz. (28 gm) flour
8 fl. ozs. (227 ml) beef broth, bouillon
4 fl. ozs. (114 ml) cream
salt and pepper to taste

Peel outer skin from kidneys and soak in cold water for 1 hour. Cut into small pieces. Fry bacon until crisp, drain and crumble. Set aside. Fry onions in butter for 3 minutes. Add chopped kidneys and fry for 5 minutes. Lower heat and stir in mushrooms, paprika, mustard, salt, pepper and flour. Stir while adding beef broth and cream. Continue cooking until meat is tender. Add bacon bits and pour this hot mixture into a buttered, heatproof casserole. Spread mashed potato over top. Place under grill to lightly brown and heat thoroughly. Makes 4 good servings.

Busy Day Scalloped Potatoes

1 lb. 10 ozs. (734 gm) peeled sliced potatoes
4 ozs. (114 gm) peeled chopped onion
1 - 10.4 oz. (295 gm) tin condensed cream of mushroom soup
4 fl. ozs. (114 ml) milk
4 rashers of bacon, grilled and diced
salt and pepper to taste

For a quick, nutritious supper when time is limited and a hot meal is in order.

In a large buttered casserole dish make layers of potato and onion, seasoning each layer with salt and pepper. Blend soup and milk. Pour over the potato-onion mix in the casserole. Sprinkle with diced bacon. Cover and bake for 1 hour in oven (180°C/350°F/gas 4). Makes 4 to 5 servings.

Sauce of the poor man – a little potato with the big one.
Irish Proverb.

Mary's Scalloped Potatoes

8 large raw potatoes, peeled and thinly sliced
2 large onions, peeled and thinly sliced
12 ozs. (340 gm) dry breadcrumbs
1 teaspoon salt
1 teaspoon black pepper
2 ozs. (57 ml) butter
16 fl. ozs. (455 ml) half cream and half milk mixed

This dish can be prepared in advance, covered and set aside and reheated at serving time. It is one of those dishes in which the flavour seems to improve the second time around.

Grease a large baking dish. Make several layers using potatoes, onions, breadcrumbs, salt, pepper and butter. Pour over cream/milk mixture. Cover dish and bake for 1 hour (180°C/350°F/gas 4). Serves 6 to 8 people.

My Favourites

1½ lbs. (681 gm) peeled, cooked potatoes, diced
2 ozs. (57 gm) flour
2 ozs. (57 ml) butter
16 fl. ozs. (455 ml) milk
8 ozs. (227 gm) sharp grated cheese
2 ozs. (57 gm) grated Parmesan cheese
4 ozs. (114 gm) buttered breadcrumbs
salt and pepper to taste

For white sauce: Blend flour into melted butter. Gradually stir in milk and cook until thickened. Add cheeses, salt and pepper. Heat to melt cheese and stir in potatoes. Put in a large buttered ovenware dish. Sprinkle crumbs on top. Bake in oven for 25 minutes (200°C/400°F/gas 6). Serves 4.

Baked Potato Strips

6 medium potatoes
2 ozs. (57 ml) melted butter
1 teaspoon garlic salt
8 ozs. (227 gm) crushed cornflakes

This makes a nice change from chips or french fries. They go with everything.

Peel and cut potatoes lengthwise into eights. Add garlic salt to crushed cornflakes. Dip potato pieces into melted butter and then into cornflakes. Place on a greased baking sheet and bake for 1 hour (180°C/350°F/gas 4). Makes 4 to 6 servings.

Crispy Ham Croquettes

1 - 6½ oz. (84 gm) pkt. instant mashed potato
12 ozs. (340 gm) chopped cooked ham
4 ozs. (114 gm) chutney or pickle relish
2 ozs. (57 ml) butter
4 ozs. (114 gm) crushed cornflakes
4 ozs. (114 gm) dry breadcrumbs
1 - 1 oz. (28 gm) envelope instant cheese sauce mix

You can use either cheese sauce or cream sauce as a topping.

Prepare instant mashed potato as instructed, but reduce water to 10 fl. ozs. so the mixture is very thick. Mix in chopped ham and chutney. Shape into balls. Melt butter in a shallow baking pan. Roll the ham-potato balls in the butter, then in the crumbs. Place back in the baking pan and bake in oven for 20 to 25 minutes (200°C/400°F/gas 6). Serve with cheese/white sauce. Serves 6.

Cottage Potatoes

16 ozs. (454 gm) cold, cooked mashed potatoes
2 ozs. (57 ml) melted butter
2 eggs, beaten
4 fl. ozs. (114 ml) cream
4 fl. ozs. (114 ml) milk

When time is short this casserole is quick and delicious. It can be served with meat or fish dishes.

Beat together potatoes, butter, eggs, cream and milk. Pour into a greased baking dish and bake uncovered for 20 to 25 minutes (180°C/350°F/gas 4). Serves 4.

Golden Peanut Potatoes

6 medium potatoes, peeled and sliced
2 ozs. (57 ml) butter
4 ozs. (114 gm) cornflake crumbs
4 ozs. (114 gm) shelled, crushed peanuts
1 teaspoon garlic or onion salt

Combine cornflake crumbs, peanuts and garlic salt in a small bowl. Melt butter in a small saucepan. Roll potato pieces in the melted butter, then in the peanut-crumb mixture. Arrange in a shallow pan and bake in oven for 50 minutes (200°C/400°F/gas 6), or until tender. Serves 4 to 6.

Crunch Top Potatoes

4 large potatoes, peeled and cut into ½ inch slices
3 ozs. (85 ml) butter
8 ozs. (227 gm) crushed cornflakes
4 ozs. (114 gm) shredded cheddar cheese
1 teaspoon paprika
1 teaspoon sugar

Melt butter in a large oven-proof pan at 180°C/350°F/ gas 4. Add potatoes and stir to coat with melted butter. Blend remaining ingredients together. Sprinkle over potatoes and return to oven for 30 minutes. Serves 4 to 6 people.

Potatoes are good when the white flower is on them,
They are better when the white foam is on them,
They are still better when the stomach is full of them.
                                        Irish Saying.

Prata na hEireann
(The Irish Potato)

I'll give you a song, 'tis a true Irish strain.
Our crúiscíns and glasses my boy let us drain.
Our voices in chorus now manfully lend
And sing the potato's the Irishman's friend.
With my Ballinamona oró, a laughing potato for me!

'Tis the root of all roots and that everyone knows
And best of all places in Ireland it grows,
So grateful of care it repays well our toil,
And like a true Paddy is fond of the soil.
With my Ballinamona oró, a mealy potato for me.

'Tis said that from Quito to Europe it came,
To Spain first imported, pappa it's name
Not amiss, for well bedded or early or late
Prolific it is and its family great.
With my Ballinamona oró, a lumping potato for me.

Práta na hÉireann, the Irish potato
It's progeny various would puzzle a saint,
Pink, purple and white, red, russet and black,
But all the same hue, with no coat on their back.
With my Ballinamona oró, the land of potatoes for me.

Nineteenth-century ballad.

SKILLET RECIPES

"Sublime potatoes! that, from Antrim's shore
To famous Kerry, form the poor man's store;
Agreeing well with every place and state –
The peasant's noggin, or the rich man's plate.
Much prized when smoking from the teeming pot,
Or in turf-embers roasted crisp and hot.
Welcome, although you be our only dish;
Welcome, companion to flesh, fowl, or fish;
But to the real gourmands, the learned few,
Most welcome, steaming in an Irish stew."
Thomas Crofton Crocker (1798-1854)

Chips

6 potatoes
cooking oil
salt
malt vinegar

Perhaps the best-known recipe of all!

Peel and wash potatoes, slice lengthwise and cut each slice into long strips. Dry potatoes on a clean cloth. Heat oil or fat in a deep fryer or in a deep heavy pan until hot for frying. Add potatoes and cook for 5 or 6 minutes. When chips are cooked they will float to the top. Remove with a slotted spoon and drain on paper. Add salt and a sprinkle of vinegar to taste. Makes 4 servings.

Penny Cakes

16 ozs. (454 gm) cooked mashed potatoes
6 ozs. (171 gm) quick cooking oatmeal
2 ozs. (57 ml) melted butter or margarine
1 oz. (28 ml) melted bacon fat

Fine fare for a cold day.

Mix the above ingredients together. Flour board with oatmeal and flour. Roll or press dough to ½ inch thickness. Cut into circles. Fry in a hot greased frying pan. Serve hot with salt and pepper, or honey, or jam. Makes 4 to 6 servings.

Boxty

10 ozs. (280 gm) peeled raw potato
10 ozs. (280 gm) cooked mashed potato
16 ozs. (454 gm) flour
1 teaspoon bread soda
3 ozs. (85 ml) bacon fat or melted butter
milk
salt, pepper to taste

Boxty is a very old Irish recipe, traditionally associated with Hallowe'en, All Hallows' Eve and All Saints Day.

In a bowl grate raw potato. Drain off as much liquid as possible and set aside. Place grated potato in another bowl and cover with cooked potato. Set aside. When the starch has sunk to the bottom of the bowl of potato liquid spill off the water and spread starch evenly over the potatoes. Mix flour, bread soda, salt and pepper and add to potato mixture. Pour melted fat on top. Mix well, adding enough milk to make a pouring batter. Heat and lightly grease a large pan. Pour spoonfuls of batter on pan. Cook on both sides until golden brown. Serve hot with butter, salt and pepper to taste. Makes 6 servings.

Judy's Pies

5 medium size potatoes, peeled, cooked and mashed
1 egg
4 ozs. (114 gm) flour
1 teaspoon baking powder
1 teaspoon caraway seeds
1 medium onion, peeled and chopped finely
milk

Mix the above ingredients in a medium-sized bowl. Thin this batter with a little milk if necessary. Heat frying pan with enough fat to cover bottom. Drop spoonfuls of batter in pan and flatten with the back of a floured spoon. Fry for 10 minutes. Turn to lightly brown other side. Serve with butter, salt and pepper to season. Makes 4 to 6 servings. Omit caraway seeds if you do not care for them.

Country Breakfast

6 potatoes, peeled, cooked and cubed
8 to 10 rashers of bacon, chopped
1 medium onion, peeled and chopped finely
4 large eggs
4 ozs. (114 gm) cheddar cheese

This quick-and-easy recipe is great if you have guests for breakfast. They will think you have been in the kitchen since sunrise preparing this delicious meal.

In a large frying pan cook bacon and onion. Set aside and keep warm. Add potatoes to pan and cook until lightly browned. Make four dents in the fried potato with the back of a large spoon. Drop an egg into each hollow, cover pan and cook until eggs are done.

Remove lid and sprinkle with bacon, onion and cheese. Replace cover and heat until cheese is melted. Slice into pie-shaped wedges. Serve hot. Makes 4 servings.

King Cormac's Pancakes

6 medium potatoes, peeled and grated
2 eggs
1 medium onion, peeled and chopped finely
1 teaspoon salt
¼ teaspoon pepper
½ teaspoon nutmeg
2 ozs. (57 gm) flour
2 fl. ozs. (57 ml) cooking oil
1 oz. (28 ml) butter

Beat eggs in a large bowl. Stir in grated, raw potato, onion, salt, pepper and nutmeg. Sprinkle with flour over top. Stir into batter. Melt oil and butter in a large heavy frying pan. Heat. Drop potato mixture in the fat by spoonfuls. Flatten each pancake with the back of a spoon dipped in flour. Fry, turning once. Delicious served with marmalade and butter. Makes 6 servings.

Hash Browns

4 large potatoes, peeled
1 oz. (28 ml) butter
1 oz. (28 ml) cooking oil
salt and pepper

Known as Hash Browns in America and Fried
Potatoes in Ireland. Either way it's a delicious accom-
paniment to eggs, bacon and sausage.

Boil potatoes for 10 minutes. Cut into cubes and fry in
frying pan using hot butter and oil. Cook until golden
brown. Season with salt and pepper. Makes 6
servings.

Friendly Potatoes

6 medium potatoes, peeled and sliced thinly
1 medium onion, peeled and chopped into small pieces
1 clove garlic, cut in half
2 tablespoons olive oil
1 oz. (28 gm) chopped parsley
2 ozs. (57 gm) choppped pimiento
1 teaspoon salt
1 tablespoon sugar
¼ teaspoon black pepper
1 chicken bouillon cube
8 fl. ozs. (227 ml) water

Fry onion and garlic in olive oil in a large frying pan.
Stir in parsley, pimiento, salt, pepper, water, bouillon,
sugar and bring to the boil. Remove garlic. Add the
sliced potatoes to the mixture and simmer until
potatoes are tender. Makes 6 servings.

Potato and Ham Patties

8 ozs. (227 gm) cooked mashed potatoes
1 lb. (454 gm) cooked ham, chopped finely
1 tablespoon chopped onion
½ teaspoon English mustard
1 fl. oz. (28 ml) cream
1 egg, beaten
4 ozs. (114 gm) dry breadrumbs
2 fl. ozs. (57 ml) cooking oil

Combine ground ham, mashed potatoes, onion and mustard in a large bowl. Blend cream and egg. Shape meat into patties and dip into egg mixture and then into breadcrumbs. Fry patties until golden brown. Serve with a cream sauce. Makes 4 to 6 servings.

Cod Fish Balls

8 medium peeled, diced potatoes
12 ozs. (340 gm) dried salted codfish
2 teaspoons butter
2 eggs, separated
fat or oil for frying

Soak fish overnight in cold water. To prepare recipe boil cod with the potatoes until tender. Drain and mash both together. Add butter and beat. Add egg yolks and beat well once more. Cool mixture and place in refrigerator to chill. Remove bowl when mixture is thoroughly chilled. Beat egg whites and fold into mix. Heat fat in a large frying pan. Drop mixture by spoonfuls into hot fat and fry until golden brown. Serve with ketchup or tartare sauce. Makes 6 servings.

BAKED JACKET POTATOES

King Spud

We praise all the flowers that we fancy
    Sip the nectar of fruit ere they're peeled,
Ignoring the common old tater
    When, in fact, he's King of the Field.
Let us show the old boy we esteem him,
    Sort of dig him up out of the mud;
Let us show him he shares our affections
    And crown him with glory – King Spud

Roquefort Stuffed Potato

6 large potatoes
2 ozs. (57 ml) melted butter
2 fl. ozs. (57 ml) fresh cream
2 - 3 oz. (85 gm each) pkts. cream cheese, softened
2 ozs. (57 ml) crumbled Roquefort cheese
2 ozs. (57 gm) minced chives

The Roquefort blended with the cream cheese and other ingredients produces a very subtle and delicious taste.

Bake potatoes in oven (180°C/350°F/gas 4) for 30 to 40 minutes depending on size. When cooked cut each potato in half lengthwise. Remove pulp to a mixing bowl. Reserve skins. Mash potato well, adding melted butter, cream, cream cheese, Roquefort cheese, and chives. Stuff the potato skins with this mixture. Place on an ovenware tray. Return to oven for 15 to 20 minutes. Makes 6 servings, 2 halves per person.

Spinach and Cheese Potatoes

6 large baked potatoes
12 ozs. (340 gm) cooked spinach, well drained
1 egg
1 - 3 oz. (85 gm) pkt cream cheese, softened
1 oz. (28 gm) grated Parmesan cheese
1 tablespoon sugar
½ teaspoon nutmeg
½ teaspoon pepper
½ teaspoon salt

Bake potatoes in oven (180°C/350°F/gas 4) for 30 to 40 minutes depending on size. When cooked cut each potato in half lengthwise. Reserve skins. Remove pulp to a mixing bowl. Add spinach, egg, cream cheese, Parmesan cheese, sugar, nutmeg, pepper and salt. Mix well. Pile this mixture into the potato skins. Place on an ovenproof tray and bake in oven 25 to 30 mins. Serves 6 at 2 halves each. Delicious with steak or chops.

Bogland Baked Potatoes

3 very large potatoes
1 chicken bouillon cube
3 fl. ozs. (85 ml) boiling water
2 ozs. (57 ml) melted butter
1 - 3 oz. (85 gm) pkt cream cheese
3 tablespoons chopped green onion tops or chives
10 large stuffed green olives, chopped

Bake potatoes in the oven until tender (180°C/350°F/gas 4), about 30 to 40 minutes. When cooked cut each one in half lengthwise. Scoop out filling and place in a mixing bowl. Reserve skins. Dissolve bouillon in boiling water. Add to potato. Add melted butter, cream cheese and chopped onion tops. Mix until light and fluffy. Stuff the potato skins. Garnish each potato with the chopped green olives. Place potatoes on a baking tray and return to the oven for 15 to 20 minutes. Makes 6 servings.

Pineapple Potato Delight

6 large baked potatoes
1 - 3 oz. (85 gm) pkt. cream cheese, softened
2 ozs. (57 ml) melted butter
1 - 6 oz. (171 gm) tin crushed pineapple, drained
paprika for a garnish

This one adds drama to a dinner menu.

Bake potatoes in oven (180°C/350°F/gas 4) for 30 to 40 minutes. When cooked cut each potato in half lengthwise. Remove pulp to a mixing bowl, saving skins. Mash potato well. Add cream cheese, butter and crushed pineapple. Stuff potato skins with this mixture. Place on an ovenware tray. Sprinkle with paprika. Return to oven to heat for serving. Makes 6 servings - 2 halves per person.

Salmon Stuffed Potatoes

6 large potatoes
1 egg, beaten
3 fl. ozs. (85 ml) hot milk
½ teaspoon paprika
1 teaspoon sugar
12 ozs. (340 gm) tin salmon (remove bones and skin)
3 ozs. (85 gm) chopped onion
2 ozs. (57 ml) butter
4 ozs. (114 gm) breadcrumbs

Fry onion in half the butter and set aside. Bake potatoes (180°C/350°F/gas 4) for about 30 to 40 minutes. Remove from oven and slice in half lengthwise. Scoop out potato. Save shells. Put potato in a large bowl. Mix in egg, milk, paprika, sugar, salmon and onions. Melt the remaining butter and mix with breadcrumbs for a topping. Refill potato shells with the mixture. Sprinkle crumbs on top. Place on an ovenproof tray and return to oven for 15 to 20 minutes. Makes 6 servings.

Cheese and Sausage Jacket Potatoes

4 large baked potatoes
2 ozs. (57 gm) apple sauce
3 ozs. (85 gm) grated Swiss cheese
12 cooked sausages, sliced

Bake potatoes (180°C/350°F/gas 4) in oven for 30 to 40 minutes. Remove from the oven and slice in half lengthwise. Scoop out cooked potato. Save shells. Mash potato. Add apple sauce and Swiss cheese and mix. Refill potato shells with this mixture. Top with sliced sausage. Place on a baking tray and return to oven for 20 to 25 minutes. Makes 4 servings.

POT LUCK

The three worst things of all:
small, soft potatoes,
from that to an uncomfortable bed
and to sleep with a bad woman.

Irish Proverb.

Donegal Orange Potatoes

8 potatoes, peeled and cubed
4 fl. ozs. (114 ml) cream
2 eggs, beaten
2 ozs. (57 ml) butter, softened
grated rind of 1 orange
½ teaspoon nutmeg
1 teaspoon sugar
½ teaspoon black pepper

Delicious with fresh, grilled sea trout. The nutmeg and orange in this recipe are a great combination.

Boil potatoes in a pot until tender. Drain and mash. Beat in the cream, eggs, butter, orange rind and seasonings. Sprinkle with sugar and keep hot until serving time. Makes 6 servings.

Pot Roast and Potatoes

12 small peeled potatoes
3 lbs. (1.36 kg) boiling beef
10 fl. ozs. (284 ml) water
1 - 10.4 oz. (294 gm) tin of condensed tomato soup
1 - 10.4 oz. (294 gm) tin of condensed cream of
    mushroom soup
1 large onion, peeled and sliced
1 tablespoon sugar
2 beef bouillon cubes
½ teaspoon black pepper
4 whole cloves
3 ozs. (85 gm) flour and cold water to thicken gravy

What would a pot roast be without potatoes?

Brown beef in its own fat in a large pot. Then add
water, soups, onion, and spices. Cover and cook for
two hours. Add the potatoes and cook until they are
tender. Remove the beef and potatoes to a serving
dish and keep warm. Bring the gravy to the boil and
thicken it with a paste made from the flour and cold
water. Makes 6 servings.

Herb Buttered Potatoes with Peas

6 new potatoes
3 ozs. (85 ml) butter
½ teaspoon garlic salt
1 teaspoon mixed herbs
1 - 12 oz. (340 gm) tin of peas

The garlic, herbs and butter add a sparkling flavour to new potatoes. Serve with the meat of your choice.

In a 3-quart saucepan cook potatoes until almost tender. Drain off water. Cut potatoes in half. Leave in pan and add butter, garlic salt and herbs. Cover and simmer slowly for a few minutes. Add the drained, tinned peas, stir, heat and serve. Makes 6 servings.

Potato Dumplings

6 medium raw potatoes, peeled and grated
5 slices of white bread
1 small onion, peeled and grated
1 teaspoon parsley flakes
2 eggs, beaten
4 ozs. (114 gm) flour
salt and pepper to taste

Always a great addition to a soup or stew.

Cut crust from bread. Dispose of crust. Soak bread in cold water. Grate potatoes in a large bowl. Squeeze water from bread and add to the grated potatoes with all the other ingredients. Mix well. Form this dough into little balls and drop into boiling, salted water in a large pot. Cover pot and simmer for 10 to 15 minutes. Remove the dumplings from the water and keep warm until serving time. Makes 4 to 6 servings.

Irish Boiled Dinner

8 large potatoes
4 lbs. (1.82 kg) corned beef
1 head cabbage, cut into eight slices
8 carrots
6 onions
1 turnip

A great standby, tasty and never out of fashion.

Cover the corned beef with water in a very large pot and cook for 3 hours. Peel, slice and prepare all the vegetables. When the corned beef is cooked add the vegetables and simmer until tender. Drain off the water and serve the sliced beef and vegetables on a large platter. Butter and season as you wish. Serves 8.

Sausage-Potato Stuffing

1 lb. (454 gm) mashed potatoes
1 lb. (454 gm) bulk sausage meat
2 ozs. (57 ml) chopped onion
1 tablespoon Worcestershire sauce
8 ozs. (227 gm) dry breadcrumbs
2 ozs. (57 ml) butter

Try this for a change from the usual turkey or chicken stuffing. Potato and spices lend a new flavour to a classic stuffing.

Fry meat and onions in butter. Mix all the ingredients well and chill until cool. Makes enough for 3 to 4 lb. chicken. Double or triple recipe accordingly for larger birds.

The Potato

I'm a careless potato, and care not a pin
   How into existence I came;
If they planted me drill-wise, or dibbled me in,
   To me 't is exactly the same.
The bean and the pea may more loftily tower,
   But I care not a button for them;
Defiance I nod with my beautiful flower
   When the earth is hoed up to my stem.

Thomas Moore

DESSERT

Potato and Apple Pie

1½ lb. (681 gm) potatoes
2 lb. (900 gm) cooking apples
10 oz. (284 gm) brown sugar
3 eggs
1 lb. (454 gm) butter
10 oz. (284 gm) plain flour
1 teaspoon ginger

Cook the potatoes and half the amount of apples and sugar together. Mash with butter, ginger and 3 whole eggs. Add flour and mix to a light dough. Place in a greased floured baking tin. Peel remainder of apples. Quarter and slice them. Arrange them on top of the dough mix. Sprinkle with remaining brown sugar and add a little ginger. Cook until cake doubles in size, about 20 minutes (190°C/375°F/gas 5). When cooked turn out and sprinkle with a little ginger. Glaze slowly under grill. Serves 10 portions.

Recipe created by John Clancy, Pastry Chef, Jury's Hotel.

Potato Dessert

Potatoes work wonders in desserts and baked cakes by adding texture, richness and moisture. They can be added to cakes and pies without significantly changing the flavour. Try frying potato slices in butter, sprinkling with nutmeg, lemon juice and honey. It's an impressive dish and an example of a different dessert.

(Taken from The Fresh Fruit and Vegetable Information Centre, Bulletin No. 94)

for your own recipes

for your own recipes